CIRCUIT TRAINING HOME WORKOUTS

WHITLEY SMITH

TABLE OF CONTENT

INTRODUCTION

Circuit training is a type of exercise routine that combines resistance training with aerobic activity. It typically involves a series of exercises that are performed in a certain order and with minimal rest periods in between. The goal of circuit training is to develop overall strength, endurance and muscular endurance.

Circuit training is popular among athletes, bodybuilders and fitness enthusiasts because it is a time-efficient way to get an effective workout.It is also suitable for all fitness levels because the exercises can be adjusted in terms of intensity, duration and difficulty.

Circuit training can be done at home or in the gym using machines, weights, bodyweight exercises and even aerobic activities.

The benefits of circuit training include increased strength and endurance, improved cardiovascular fitness, and improved muscular coordination, balance and agility. Circuit training can be used to target specific muscles and can also be used as part of a weight loss program.

BENEFITS OF CIRCUIT TRAINING

- ✓ Circuit training is perfect for carrying out intense fat-burning exercises.

- ✓ It is a fantastic basic exercise to condition and strengthens the body.

- ✓ Working every muscle in your body is easy with circuit training.

- ✓ It may be adjusted for any size of working space.

- ✓ You may perform circuit training in the house; it's not necessary to use expensive gym equipment.

- ✓ It may be tailored for specificity and is simple to adapt to your sport.

- ✓ It can be used in a beginner's weight training routine.

- ✓ Circuit training is a fantastic strategy to aid with weight loss.

Numerous home weight loss programs integrate circuit training to assist you in losing weight and being in shape; here, we lay out some circuit training workouts. *Feel at liberty to alter and modify them to your specific requirements.*

BASIC CIRCUIT TRAINING WORKOUT

Skipping

There are numerous ways to keep. Jumping with both feet together is a great warm-up and a very strenuous workout.

Time: 5 minutes

Directions

✓ Pick a rope that is the appropriate length for your height.

✓ Ensure the handles of the rope are at your armpit height when you are standing in the center of it.

✓ Grab the handles, keeping your elbows near to your sides, grasp the rope's handles in each hand.

✓ Throw the rope, As the rope hits the ground, jump off of it.

✓ Landing on the soles of your feet while keeping your feet close together.

✓ While skipping, timing is crucial. When the rope is about to touch your feet, try to jump.

Please Note: If you've never skipped before**, start out gently and get comfortable practicing hopping** with the rope before even swinging it. **Start small and progress to performing complete skips.**

Try several varieties of skipping once you have perfected the fundamentals, such as attempting to cross your arms or hopping on one foot.

To avoid injury, be sure to stretch prior to as well as after skipping.

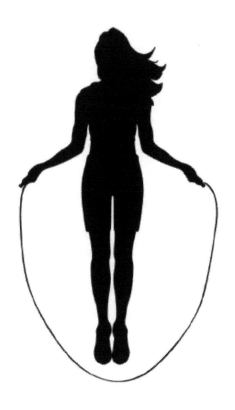

Air Squats

They are the foundation of all bodyweight exercises. They focus on **the glutes, or butt muscles, which are the biggest** muscles in the body.

Reps: 2

Direction

- ✓ Begin by assuming a standing position with your feet shoulder-width apart and your toes pointed outward.

- ✓ All through the workout, maintain a raised chest up, your core firm, and your spine in a neutral position.

- ✓ Pressing your hips back and folding your knees to lower your body to the level of sitting on a chair is how to start a squat.

- ✓ Maintain a tracking gait with your knees over your toes and your weight on your heels.

- ✓ After your thighs are level with the floor, slowly lower your body.

✓ If necessary, allow yourself a short pause at the bottom of the squat before driving through your heels to make a stand and contracting your glutes at the pinnacle of the exercise.

Push Ups

Push-ups is a combinatorial workout that engages the arms, core, triceps, and chest in addition to other upper body core muscles. They aid in enhancing the general strength and stamina of the upper body.

Push-ups is a crucial activity to include in any fitness regimen since they provide a number of health advantages and engage a variety of upper-body muscles.

Reps: 20

Directions

- ✓ Start by laying your hands flat and a little wider than shoulder-width apart on the floor. You should have your feet together.

- ✓ Ensure that your arms are fully stretched, and your head should be in line with your heels.

- ✓ Enable your body to descend toward the floor, tighten your core, and flex your elbows.

- ✓ Maintain a straight back and a low butt.

- ✓ Your chest should be almost parallel to the ground as you descend.

- ✓ Utilizing your arm and chest to raise your body, pull yourself right back to the beginning position while maintaining the same position for your hands.

- ✓ Repeat as many times as necessary.

Star jumps/Jumping Jacks

Star jumps, also known as jumping jacks, is an aerobic exercise that involves jumping with the legs spread wide and the arms raised above the head. It is a full body workout that can help improve cardiovascular endurance, strength, and flexibility.

Reps: 20

Directions

- ✓ Stand with your feet slightly apart, your arms bent and your hands clasped in front of your chest.

- ✓ Jump up, extending your legs out to the sides and your arms up above your head.

- ✓ Quickly bring your legs back together as you bring your arms back down to chest level.

- ✓ Land on both feet, returning to your starting position.

Sit-ups

Sit-ups are a type of exercise used to strengthen and tone the core muscles of the abdomen. This exercise can be made more difficult by adding weights or resistance bands to increase the intensity. Additionally, different variations of the sit-up can be performed to target different muscles of the core. Sit-ups are a great way to strengthen the abdominal muscles and improve overall core stability and strength.

Reps: 20

Directions

✓ Start by lying flat on your back with your feet flat on the floor and your legs bent at a 90 degree angle.

✓ Put your hands at the back of your head and make your elbows wide.

✓ Engage your core and press your lower back into the ground.

- ✓ Exhale as you curl your torso up, lifting your head and shoulders off the ground.

- ✓ Inhale as you lower your torso back down to the starting position.

Crunches

Crunches are a type of abdominal exercise that strengthens and tones the abdominal muscles.

Crunches are one of the most common abdominal exercises used in core strength and conditioning programs, and they can be used to target both the upper and lower abdominal muscles.

Reps: 20

Directions

✓ Knees bent and feet flat on the floor, lie on your back. With your elbows pointed out to the sides, place your hands behind your head.

✓ Engage your core and use your abdominal muscles to lift your torso up and off the floor.

✓ Slowly lower your torso back down to the floor, stopping just before your shoulder blades touch the floor.

✓ Repeat for desired number of repetitions.

Leg Raises

Leg raises are a type of exercise used to strengthen and tone the muscles in the legs. They involve lifting the legs up and down in a controlled manner, usually with the back flat on the floor. Leg raises can be done with or without weights and with various amounts of resistance. Regularly doing leg raises can help improve strength, balance, and flexibility in the legs.

Reps: 20

Directions

✓ Lie on your back on a mat or the floor and place your arms out to the sides, palms facing down.

✓ Exhale and lift both legs off the floor until they are pointing toward the ceiling.

✓ Hold for a few seconds and then inhale as you slowly lower your legs back down to the starting position.

✓ Repeat for the desired number of repetitions.

Mountain Climbers

Mountain climbing is a high-intensity, full-body exercise that can help strengthen your core, improve your balance and coordination, and burn a lot of calories. It is beneficial for improving your cardiovascular fitness, muscular endurance, and coordination.

Time: 30 seconds

Directions

- ✓ Begin in a plank position with your shoulders over your wrists and your core engaged.

- ✓ Drive your right knee to your chest while keeping your hips low and your core tight.

- ✓ Return your right foot back to the plank position.

- ✓ Immediately drive your left knee to your chest while keeping your hips low and your core tight.

- ✓ Return your left foot back to the plank position.

- ✓ Continue alternating your legs while keeping your core engaged and your hips low.

✓ Aim to do 15–20 reps on each side.

Back Extensions

Back extensions are a type of exercise that works the muscles of the lower back and core. They are typically performed by lying on the stomach and lifting the chest, arms, and legs off the floor. This type of exercise can help strengthen the lower back and core muscles, improve posture, and increase flexibility. Back extensions can also be performed with the aid of a fitness machine, such as a back extension bench.

Reps: 20

Directions

- ✓ Start by lying face down on a mat, with your legs straight and your arms at your sides.

- ✓ Lift your head and chest off the floor, arching your back as much as you can. Hold for a few seconds and then lower your body back to the starting position.

- ✓ To make the exercise more difficult, you can add a weight to your chest or back. Hold the weight with your hands or place it between your shoulder blades.

Please Note: To make the exercise easier, you can perform the exercise while lying on an exercise ball. The instability of the ball will make the exercise easier.

Burpees

Burpees are an intense full body exercise that primarily works the muscles of the legs and core. This exercise involves starting from a standing position, dropping into a squat, kicking your feet back, doing a pushup, jumping back into a squat, and then jumping into the air. This exercise is often done for time and can be modified for different fitness levels.

For a more intense workout, try adding weights or doing a burpee with a jump at the end.

Reps: 10

Directions

- ✓ Put your feet hip-width apart and stand up straight.

- ✓ Squat down and place your hands on the floor in front of you.

- ✓ Kick your feet back into a plank position.

- ✓ Immediately lower your chest and thighs to the floor by bending your elbows.

- ✓ Push yourself back up to the plank position by straightening your arms.

- ✓ Jump your feet back in towards your hands.

- ✓ Stand up and jump into the air with your arms overhead.

- ✓ Land and repeat the sequence.

High Knees

High Knees is a calisthenics exercise that involves running in place while raising your knees as high as you can. This exercise is meant to improve the power and endurance of your muscles, as well as your cardiovascular system.

High Knees can be performed as a standalone exercise, or as part of a larger workout routine.

Time: 30 seconds

Directions

- ✓ Stand up straight with your feet shoulder-width apart.

- ✓ Bring one knee up toward your chest as high as you can.

- ✓ Immediately switch legs and bring the other knee up.

- ✓ Continue alternating legs, bringing your knees up as quickly as possible.

- ✓ Keep your core engaged and your back straight throughout the exercise.

- ✓ Try to keep your arms at your sides, but you can use them for balance if needed.

- ✓ Aim for at least 10 reps of high knees on each side.

- ✓ Increase the speed and/or reps as you get stronger.

Plank

Plank is an exercise that strengthens the core muscles by holding your body in a straight line position, as if you were doing a push-up. You hold this position for a certain amount of time, typically 30 seconds to one minute, in order to train your core muscles.

Plank can be done with the hands placed on the floor, elbows tucked in to the sides, or with the forearms and elbows on the floor. It can also be done with the arms extended out to the sides, or with the arms and legs in a push-up position.

Time: 30 seconds

Directions

- ✓ Get into a pushup position on the floor with your arms straight, palms flat, and elbows directly beneath your shoulders.

- ✓ Engage your core and glutes to keep your back straight and your body in a straight line.

✓ Hold this position for 30 seconds to 1 minute, working up to 2 to 3 minutes as you get stronger.

✓ To make the exercise more challenging, you can raise one foot off the floor, or hold the plank on your elbows instead of your hands.

✓ Keep your neck and shoulders relaxed and your gaze focused on the floor.

Tricep Dips

Tricep dips are an upper body exercise that primarily target the triceps muscles. It is a bodyweight exercise that can be performed anywhere, with or without equipment.

Tricep dips are a great exercise for toning and strengthening the triceps muscles, as well as the chest, shoulders, and core.

Reps: 20

Directions

- ✓ Begin by sitting on the edge of a sturdy chair or bench, with your hands placed shoulder-width apart on the edge of the seat.

- ✓ Straighten your arms and slowly lift your body off the seat, keeping your arms locked out.

- ✓ Slowly lower your body towards the floor until your elbows are bent at a 90-degree angle.

- ✓ Push your body back up to the starting position.

Jumping Squats

Jumping squats are an explosive plyometric exercise that targets the entire lower body. It is an effective and challenging exercise that can help you build power and strength in your legs.

Reps: 20

Directions

- ✓ Stand with your feet hip-width apart and your hands by your sides.

- ✓ Squat down by bending your knees.

- ✓ Explode off the ground and jump as high as you can.

- ✓ Land softly and immediately lower back into a squat position.

Wall Sit

A wall sit is an isometric exercise that involves sitting against a wall with your back and thighs parallel to the ground and your feet shoulder width apart. It is used to strengthen the muscles of the hips, thighs, and core.

Time: 30 seconds

Directions

- ✓ Stand with your back against a wall and your feet shoulder width apart.

- ✓ Bend your knees and slide down the wall until your thighs are parallel to the ground and your knees are bent at a 90-degree angle.

- ✓ Hold this position for as long as you can, aiming for at least 30 seconds.

- ✓ Slowly slide back up the wall to return to the starting position.

Jogging

Jogging is a form of physical exercise that involves running at a slow and steady pace. It is usually done for recreational or fitness purposes. Jogging is often used as a form of aerobic exercise, as it helps to improve your cardiovascular fitness and reduce the risk of developing certain health conditions.

Time: 5 minutes

Directions

- ✓ Wear comfortable, supportive shoes.

- ✓ Warm up with light stretching or a brisk walk for 5 minutes.

- ✓ Start jogging slowly, at a pace that is comfortable for you.

- ✓ Increase your speed gradually as you become more comfortable.

- ✓ Try to maintain a steady pace for at least 15-20 minutes.

✓ Cool down with a light stretch or a walk for 5 minutes.

✓ Repeat 2-3 times per week.

Glute Bridges

Glute Bridges, also known as hip thrusts, is a popular exercise used to strengthen and tone the glutes, hamstrings, and core muscles. Then, you raise your hips up towards the sky, hold the position for a few seconds, and then lower your hips back down to the ground. This exercise can be done with or without weights, and can also be progressed by adding bands or variations such as single-leg glute bridges.

Reps: 20

Directions

- ✓ Start by lying on your back with your knees bent and feet flat on the ground, with your arms outstretched to the sides.

- ✓ Keeping your core engaged, press your feet into the ground and lift your hips up towards the sky.

✓ Hold the top position for a few seconds, and then slowly lower your hips back down to the ground.

Reverse Lunges

Reverse lunges are a lower body exercise that strengthens and tones the muscles of the legs. This exercise is performed by standing with your feet hip-width apart. Then, step one leg back and lower the hips down towards the floor. Push off the front foot to stand back up and repeat the same motion with the opposite leg. Reverse lunges can be performed with or without weights, and can be progressed by adding bands or variations such as curtsy lunges.

Reps: 20

Directions

- ✓ Start by standing with your feet hip-width apart and your arms outstretched to the sides.

- ✓ Step one leg back and lower the hips down towards the floor, keeping your front knee over your front ankle.

- ✓ Push off the front foot to stand back up, and then repeat the same motion with the opposite leg.

✓ Repeat for the desired number of repetitions.

Bicycle Crunches

Bicycle crunches are a core exercise that targets the rectus abdominis (abs) muscles. The exercise is performed by lying on the back with the hands behind the head and the legs raised in the air. The exercise consists of alternating bringing each elbow up towards the opposite knee. This is done in a pedaling motion, hence the name "bicycle crunches".

Reps: 20

Directions

- ✓ Start by lying on your back with your hands behind your head and your legs raised in the air.

- ✓ Bend your right knee and bring it towards your chest while you also bring your left elbow towards the right knee.

✓ Return to the starting position and repeat with the opposite leg and arm.

✓ Continue alternating sides in a pedaling motion until you have completed the desired number of repetitions.

✓ Be sure to keep your lower back pressed against the floor throughout the exercise.

Superman

Supermans is an exercise that works the muscles of the back. It is an isometric, or static, exercise and can be performed without any equipment. The exercise involves lying on the stomach and then raising the arms and legs at the same time, in a superman-like pose. This exercise works the muscles of the lower and upper back, as well as the glutes.

Reps: 20

Directions

- ✓ Lie face down on the floor.

- ✓ Place your arms out in front of you, palms facing down.

- ✓ Raise your arms and legs at the same time, so that your body is in a superman-like pose.

- ✓ Hold this position for 10-15 seconds.

✓ Return to the starting position and repeat until you have completed the desired number of repetitions.

Shoulder Taps

Shoulder taps are an exercise that targets the deltoids, or shoulder muscles. The exercise involves getting into a plank position and then tapping the opposite shoulder with the hand. This exercise can be done for time, or for a certain number of repetitions, and can be modified for all fitness levels.

Reps: 10

Directions

- ✓ Begin in a plank position, with your arms straight, your hands directly under your shoulders and your feet hip width apart.

- ✓ Touch your left shoulder with your right hand while raising it.

- ✓ Go back to the beginning, then repeat on the opposite side.

- ✓ Continue alternating sides, tapping your shoulder with the opposite hand.

✓ Make sure your body remains in a straight line throughout the exercise, and your core is engaged.

Russian Twists

Russian twists are a core exercise that targets the obliques and the rectus abdominis (abs). The exercise is performed while sitting on the floor with the legs bent and the feet off the ground. The exercise consists of twisting the torso side to side while holding a medicine ball, dumbbell or weight plate. This exercise can be done for time or for a certain number of repetitions.

Reps: 20

Directions

- ✓ Sit on the floor with your legs bent and your feet off the ground.

- ✓ Holding a medicine ball, dumbbell or weight plate, twist your torso to the left side, bringing the weight across your body.

- ✓ Then, repeat on the other side while returning to your starting position.

- ✓ Continue alternating sides, twisting your torso from side to side.

✓ Make sure your core is engaged throughout the exercise.

CONCLUSION

In conclusion, circuit training home exercises can be a great way to get a full-body workout without having to go to the gym. It is a time-efficient way to get a full-body workout that can help you build strength and endurance.

Furthermore, it can be tailored to fit your individual needs and preferences, making it a great option for anyone. With the right equipment, knowledge, and motivation, circuit training can be an effective way to reach your fitness goals.

We hope this information has been helpful in helping you to understand the benefits of circuit training home exercises. We hope you find the right exercises that are suitable for your individual needs and preferences and that you have a great time while being healthy and fit.

Made in United States
Troutdale, OR
02/23/2024

17933431R00031